Rookie
Read-About® Health

Take Care of Your Teeth

By Don L. Curry

Consultant
Nanci R. Vargus, Ed.D.
Assistant Professor of Literacy
University of Indianapolis, Indianapolis, Indiana

Children's Press®
A Division of Scholastic Inc.
New York   Toronto   London   Auckland   Sydney
Mexico City   New Delhi   Hong Kong
Danbury, Connecticut

Designer: Herman Adler Design
Photo Researcher: Caroline Anderson
The photo on the cover shows a boy talking to his dentist.

Library of Congress Cataloging-in-Publication Data

Curry, Don L.
  Take care of your teeth / by Don L. Curry.
    p. cm. — (Rookie read-about health)
  Includes index.
  ISBN 0-516-25875-3 (lib. bdg.)   0-516-27915-7 (pbk.)
  1. Teeth—Care and hygiene—Juvenile literature. I. Title. II. Series.
  RK63.C875 2005
  617.6'01—dc22
                            2004015301

CHILDREN'S PRESS, and ROOKIE READ-ABOUT®,
and associated logos are trademarks and or registered trademarks
of Scholastic Library Publishing. SCHOLASTIC and associated logos
are trademarks and or registered trademarks of Scholastic Inc.

1 2 3 4 5 6 7 8 9 10 R 14 13 12 11 10 09 08 07 06 05

Why do you need to take care of your teeth?

4

Your teeth help you eat. They help you talk. They help you smile!

You start out with 20
"baby" teeth.

Those teeth fall out and
new ones grow. The
new teeth are called
permanent teeth.

This girl has lost a "baby" tooth.

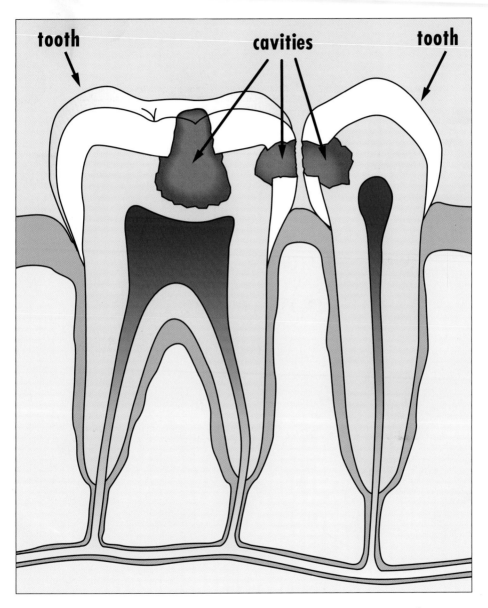

You must keep your teeth healthy.

Brush your teeth and rinse your mouth with water. If you don't brush your teeth, you can get cavities.

Cavities are holes in your teeth.

Enamel is the hard outside part of your teeth. It protects them.

You get cavities when something eats the enamel. Plaque (plak) eats the enamel on your teeth.

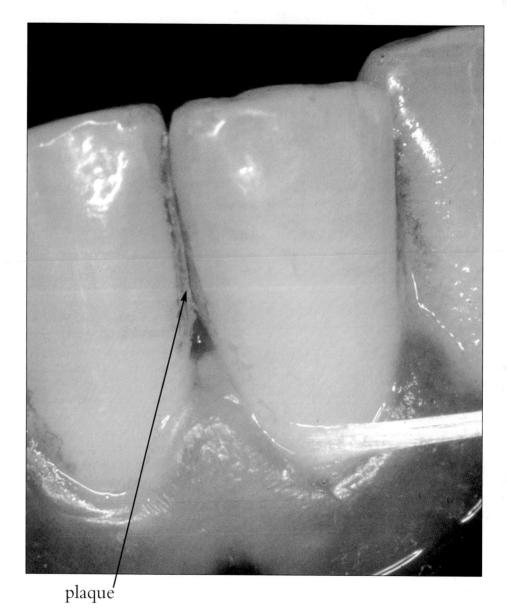

plaque

11

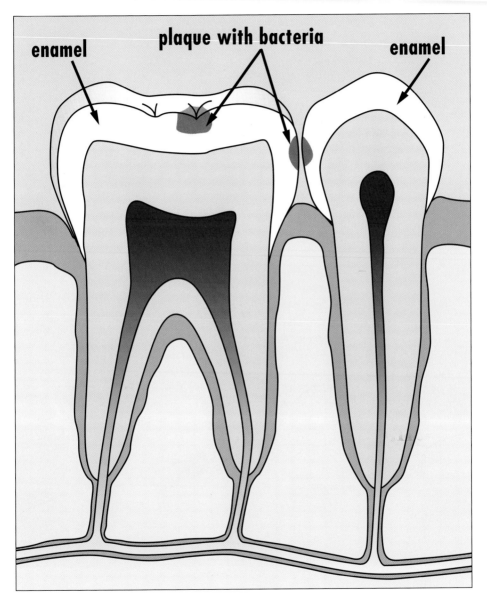

Plaque is a clear film that sticks to your teeth. Plaque has bacteria in it.

Bacteria are tiny living things. Bacteria turn sugar into acid. The acid eats the enamel on your teeth.

Brushing your teeth gets rid of plaque.

You should brush your teeth at least two times a day.

Brush your teeth after you eat. Brush your teeth before you go to bed, too.

bristles

16

Use a toothbrush with soft bristles. Bristles that are too hard can hurt your gums.

Your gums are pink. They hold your teeth in place.

Use a little bit of toothpaste when you brush your teeth.

Always spit out the toothpaste and rinse your mouth with water. It is not good to swallow toothpaste.

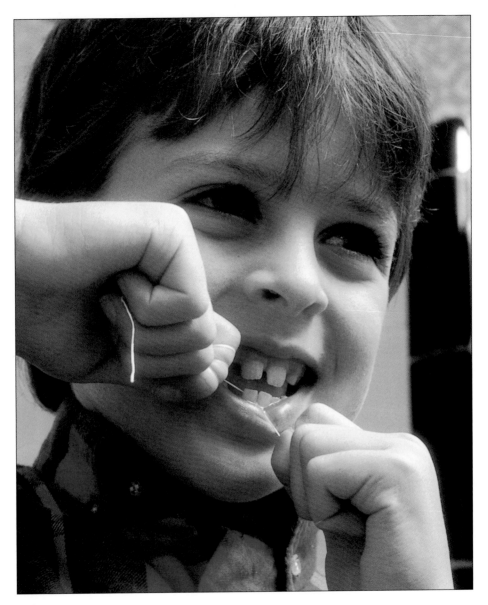

You can clean your teeth with dental floss, too.

After you brush your teeth, you should floss. Flossing gets rid of the food you miss when you brush.

Don't eat too many starchy or sweet foods.

Remember that plaque has bacteria in it. Bacteria turns sugar into acid. Acid eats the enamel on your teeth.

Then, you'll get cavities.

These girls are buying candy. Candy has sugar in it.

23

These people are eating a healthy dinner.

24

Eat fresh fruits and vegetables. Drink milk, too. These foods are good for your teeth.

They have vitamins and minerals in them.

Go to your dentist two times a year.

Dentists look for cavities and gum disease. They can fix teeth that have cavities.

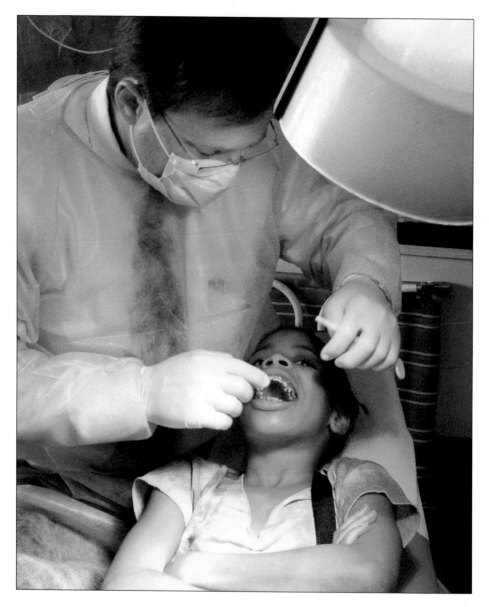

Take good care of
your teeth.

Then you will have
something to smile about!

Words You Know

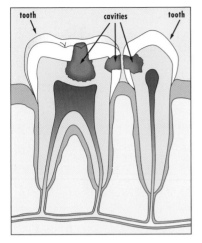

cavity

dental floss

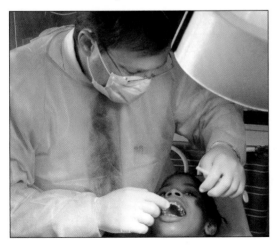

dentist

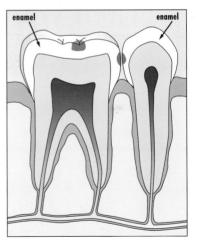

enamel

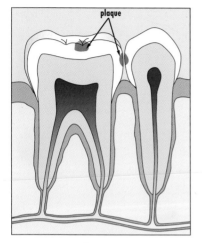

plaque

smile

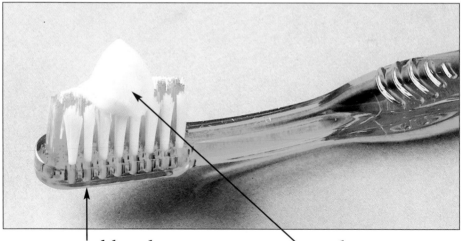

toothbrush   toothpaste

Index

About the Author

Don L. Curry is a writer, editor, and consultant who lives and works in New York City. He has written more than 30 nonfiction books about science. The study of the human body is by far his favorite topic. When Don is not writing, he can be found reading in Central Park or riding his bike on the streets of "the greatest city on Earth."

Photo Credits

Photographs © 2005: Corbis Images: 24 (Rob Lewine), 15 (Royalty-Free); Index Stock Imagery: 7 (CLEO Freelance), 19 (Image Source Limited); Masterfile/Gary Rhijnsburger: cover; Peter Arnold Inc./Dr. R. Gottsegen: 11; Photo Researchers, NY: 3 (Aaron Haupt), 20, 30 top right (Ken Lax); PhotoEdit/Spencer Grant: 16, 31 bottom; Stock Boston/Bill Bachmann: 28; The Image Works: 4, 31 top right (Bob Daemmrich), 27, 30 bottom left (Jim West); Visuals Unlimited/Jeff Greenberg: 23.

Illustrations by Bob Italiano